# Having Fun

Vicki Yates

D0528793

**www.heinemann.co.uk/library**
Visit our website to find out more information about Heinemann Library books.

To order:
☎ Phone 44 (0) 1865 888066
📄 Send a fax to 44 (0) 1865 314091
💻 Visit the Heinemann Bookshop at www.heinemann.co.uk/library to browse our catalogue and order online.

First published in Great Britain by Heinemann Library, Halley Court, Jordan Hill, Oxford OX2 8EJ, part of Pearson Education. Heinemann is a registered trademark of Pearson Education Ltd.

Editorial: Charlotte Guillain and Vicki Yates
Design: Victoria Bevan, Joanna Hinton-Malivoire and Q2A solutions
Picture research: Ruth Blair and Q2A solutions
Production: Duncan Gilbert

Printed and bound in China by South China Printing Co. Ltd.

ISBN 978 0431 19185 0 (Hardback)

ISBN 978 0431 19193 5 (Paperback)
13 12 11 10 09
10 9 8 7 6 5 4 3 2 1

**British Library Cataloguing in Publication Data**
Yates, Vicki. Having fun. - (Then and now)
1. Recreation - Juvenile literature 2. Recreation - History - Juvenile literature
790
A full catalogue record for this book is available from the British Library.

**Acknowledgements**
The publishers would like to thank the following for permission to reproduce photographs: Alamy pp. **9** (Martin Harvey), **11** (Steve Skjold), **19** (Mike Watson Images), **22** (Arthur Steel; Comstock Images p. **23**; Corbis pp. **10** (Owen Franken), **18** (Hulton-Deutsch Collection); Flickr p. **13** (Jimmy McDonald); Getty Images p. **20** (Paul Martin/General Photographic Agency); Irish Press Archives p. **5** (Thérèse Sheehy-Devine); Istockphoto pp. **7**, **23**; Library of Congress pp. **8**, **12**; Photolibrary.com pp. **6** (Index Stock Imagery), **15** (Franck Dunouau/Photononstop), **21** (Dynamic Graphics); Science & Society p. **16** (NMPFT Daily Herald Archive), **17** (Ian Hooton/Science Photo Library); Shutterstock pp. **4** (Alex Melnick), **23**; Staffordshire County Records Office pp. **14**, **23**

Cover photograph of boy with hula hoop reproduced with permission of Getty Images (Photodisc Blue) and photo of boy playing football reproduced with permission of Corbis (Jim Cummins). Back cover photograph reproduced with permission of Irish Press Archives (Therese Sheehy-Devine).

Every effort has been made to contact copyright holders of any material reproduced in this book. Any omissions will be rectified in subsequent printings if notice is given to the publishers.

# Contents

# Having fun

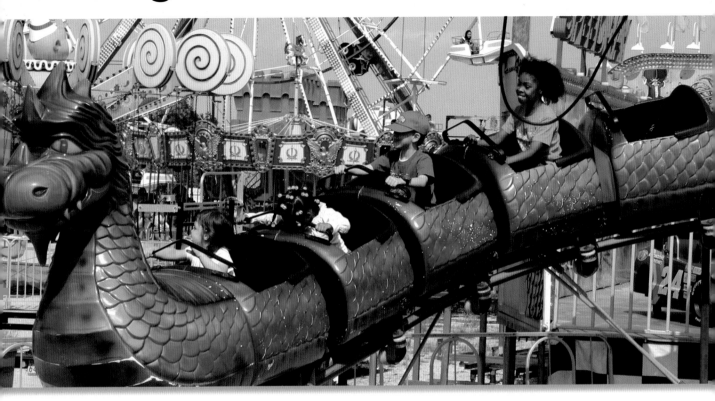

Everyone likes to have fun.

It makes us feel happy.

Long ago people liked to have fun, too.

# Toys and games

Long ago people played board games.

Today people can play computer games.

Long ago people moved toys
by hand.

Today some toys move by
remote control.

Long ago toys were made of wood or metal.

Today toys can be made
of plastic.

Long ago children played outside.

Today children have fun
outside, too.

# Entertainment

Long ago people watched plays.

Today people can watch films, too.

Long ago people listened to the radio.

Today people can watch
television, too.

Long ago people listened to records.

Today we can listen to CDs.

# Let's compare

Long ago people had fun in different ways.

Which is better? Then or now?

# What is it?

Long ago children played with this toy.
Do you know what it is?

Answer on p. 24

# Picture glossary

**CD** compact disc. A small plastic disc that has music on it.

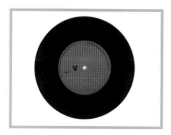

**play** story told at the theatre

**record** black plastic disc that has music on it

**remote control** machine used to control something from a distance, such as a toy or a television set

# Index

**Answer to question on p. 22:** It is a hoop and stick game. Children rolled the hoop with the stick.

**Note to Parents and Teachers**

**Before reading**
Tell the children about the games you used to play when you were at school. If possible show them such games as hopscotch, jacks and marbles. Ask them what their favourite games are. What do they play when they get home?

**After reading**
• Make a collection in the classroom of older toys and games. Ask the children if their parents or grandparents have any toys they played with. Talk about the differences between these toys and today's toys.
• Show the children how to play simple board games such as Snakes and Ladders, Ludo and marbles.